3 Days Guide to Bu
Hungary

Budapest (Image Credit: Dimitris Kamaras, Flickr cc)

Welcome to the Budapest Travel Guide, a comprehensive resource designed to help you plan the perfect trip to one of Europe's most vibrant and exciting cities. Budapest, the capital of Hungary, is a city that is steeped in history and culture, with a rich heritage that is reflected in its stunning architecture, world-class museums, and vibrant arts scene.

Our guide has been designed to help you make the most of your time in Budapest, whether you have just a few days or a few weeks to explore this amazing city. We've put together a detailed itinerary that highlights the must-see sights, hidden gems, and best local experiences, so that you can make the most of your time here. We've also included practical tips and information on everything from getting around the city to finding the best restaurants and hotels.

Budapest is a city that has something for everyone, from its thermal baths and picturesque parks, to its bustling markets and vibrant nightlife. It's a city that is both dynamic and sophisticated, with a rich cultural heritage that is sure to enchant and inspire you.

So, whether you're here to explore the history and culture, to soak up the local atmosphere, or just to relax and unwind, we hope that this travel guide will be your ultimate companion on your journey to Budapest. Let's get started and discover all that this magical city has to offer!

I. Introduction

Welcome to Budapest, one of Europe's most charming and vibrant cities! Whether you're a first-time visitor or a seasoned traveler, this guide is designed to help you make the most of your trip to Hungary's capital, even if you only have three days to spare.

Budapest is a city of contrasts, with a rich history, stunning architecture, and a lively cultural scene. It's also known for its thermal baths, delicious cuisine, and buzzing nightlife. With so much to see and do, planning a trip to Budapest can be overwhelming. That's why we've created this comprehensive guide, to help you make the most of your time in the city.

In this guide, we'll take you through the best places to visit in Budapest, including the must-see landmarks, the most interesting neighborhoods, and the top local events and festivals. We'll also give you practical information on getting around the city, where to stay, and how to make the most of your budget.

So, whether you're interested in history, art, food, or just soaking in the local atmosphere, we've got you covered. Let's dive in and discover the best of Budapest!

A. Why Visit Budapest

Budapest is one of Europe's most beautiful and exciting cities, with a rich history, stunning architecture, and a lively cultural scene. Whether you're interested in exploring the city's landmarks, soaking in thermal baths, indulging in delicious Hungarian cuisine, or simply strolling through charming neighborhoods, Budapest has something to offer for every traveler. Here are some unique views that you may not have known about:

- Budapest is often referred to as the "Paris of the East" for its romantic atmosphere, grand boulevards, and beautiful bridges over the Danube River. But it's also a city with a distinctive identity, blending Eastern and Western cultures in a unique way.

- The city is home to more than 100 thermal springs, which have been used for healing purposes since Roman times. Today, Budapest is famous for its historic thermal baths, such as the Széchenyi and Gellért Baths, where you can soak in mineral-rich waters and relax in a beautiful setting.

- Budapest has a vibrant cultural scene, with world-class museums, galleries, and theaters. The Hungarian National Museum, the Museum of Fine Arts, and the Hungarian State Opera House are just a few of the must-visit cultural institutions in the city.

- The city is a foodie's paradise, with a rich culinary tradition that combines Hungarian, Jewish, and Austrian influences. From hearty goulash to sweet chimney cakes, Budapest has a variety of delicious dishes to try.

- Budapest is also a city of contrasts, with a mix of grand historic buildings and quirky, bohemian neighborhoods. The Jewish Quarter, with its famous ruin bars, is a great example of this unique blend of styles.

With so much to see and do, Budapest is a city that is sure to capture your imagination and leave a lasting impression. So, whether you're interested in history, culture, food, or just soaking in the local atmosphere, Budapest is the perfect destination for you!

B. Essential Information

Before you visit Budapest, it's important to know some essential information that will help you plan your trip. Here are some key things to keep in mind:

1. Language: Hungarian is the official language of Hungary, but most people in Budapest speak English, especially those in the tourism industry.
2. Currency: The official currency of Hungary is the Hungarian Forint (HUF). Euros are also widely accepted in many tourist areas, but it's always best to carry some Hungarian Forints with you.
3. Visa Requirements: If you're a citizen of the European Union, the United States, Canada, Australia, or New Zealand, you don't need a visa to visit Hungary for up to 90 days. If you're from a different country, be sure to check the visa requirements before you travel.
4. Time Zone: Budapest is in the Central European Time Zone (CET), which is one hour ahead of Coordinated Universal Time (UTC+1).
5. Electricity: The standard voltage in Hungary is 230V, and the frequency is 50Hz. The power sockets used in Budapest are Type F, which are the same as most of continental Europe.
6. Tipping: Tipping is a common practice in Budapest, especially in restaurants, bars, and for taxi rides. The standard tip is around 10% of the total bill.
7. Emergency Numbers: In case of an emergency in Budapest, dial 112 for all emergency services, including police, fire, and ambulance.

By keeping these essential information points in mind, you'll be well prepared for your trip to Budapest. With this practical knowledge, you'll be able to focus on enjoying the sights, sounds, and tastes of the city without worrying about the logistics.

C. A Brief History of Budapest

Budapest, the capital of Hungary, is a city with a rich and varied history that dates back over 2,000 years. The city has been shaped by numerous cultural influences and historical events, each leaving its mark on the city's architecture, art, and culture. In this section, we will take a closer look at the history of Budapest, from its earliest origins to the present day.

Early History

The area now known as Budapest has been inhabited since prehistoric times. The first known settlers in the area were the Celts, who established a small village on the site of present-day Buda. The village was later conquered by the Romans, who established the town of Aquincum in 89 AD. Aquincum quickly grew to become an important center of trade and commerce, and remains a popular attraction in Budapest to this day.

Medieval Times

In the 9th century, the Magyars, a nomadic tribe from Central Asia, arrived in the Carpathian Basin and established the Kingdom of Hungary. The Kingdom flourished during the medieval period, and Budapest began to take shape as an important trading and cultural center. The first written reference to Buda and Pest, the two cities that make up modern-day Budapest, dates back to the early 13th century. The two cities were located on opposite sides of the Danube River, with Buda on the west bank and Pest on the east bank.

Turkish Occupation

In the 16th century, the Ottoman Turks invaded Hungary and occupied Budapest for over 150 years. During this time, the city underwent significant changes, with many buildings being destroyed or repurposed. The Turks built several mosques and baths, many of which still exist today, and the city became an important center of Islamic culture and art.

Habsburg Rule

In the 18th century, Hungary came under Habsburg rule and became part of the Austro-Hungarian Empire. Budapest began to flourish once again, with new buildings, bridges, and monuments being constructed throughout the city. The most significant of these was the Chain Bridge, which was completed in 1849 and remains one of Budapest's most iconic landmarks.

20th Century

In the 20th century, Budapest was shaken by two World Wars, the Holocaust, and Communist rule. During World War II, the city was heavily bombed by the Allies, and many buildings and monuments were destroyed or damaged. The city also played a key role in the 1956 Hungarian Revolution, when Hungarian students and workers rose up against the Communist government.

In the years that followed, Budapest underwent significant changes, with many new buildings and monuments being constructed. In 1987, Budapest was listed as a UNESCO World Heritage Site, in recognition of its outstanding cultural and architectural heritage.

Today, Budapest is a vibrant and cosmopolitan city, with a rich history and culture that is reflected in its stunning architecture, world-class museums, and vibrant arts scene. The city continues to evolve and grow, while remaining true to its roots and the traditions that have shaped it over the centuries.

In conclusion, the history of Budapest is a long and complex one, filled with triumphs and tragedies, wars and revolutions, and cultural and artistic movements. From its early origins as a small Celtic village, to its status today as one of Europe's most dynamic and exciting cities, Budapest has undergone countless changes and transformations over the centuries. Its rich history and culture are an integral part of the city's identity and charm, and provide a fascinating glimpse into the story of this remarkable city.

D. 10 Most Important Hungarian Artists

Hungary has a rich and vibrant culture that is heavily influenced by its history and unique geographical location. From classical music to contemporary art, there are many figures who have made significant contributions to the Hungarian culture scene. Whether you're an art lover or a music enthusiast, these ten individuals have played a crucial role in shaping the culture of Hungary. In this guide, we will introduce you to the ten most important people in the culture, music, and art scene of Hungary and provide a short description of their accomplishments and contributions. Get ready to be inspired and awed by the passion and talent of these iconic individuals.

1. Béla Bartók - a famous composer, pianist, and collector of folk music who is widely regarded as one of the most significant composers of the 20th century.
2. Franz Liszt - a renowned composer and pianist who had a significant influence on the development of Western classical music.
3. Zoltán Kodály - a composer, ethnomusicologist, and educator who is known for his efforts to preserve and promote Hungarian folk music.
4. László Moholy-Nagy - an artist and photographer who was a key figure in the development of the Bauhaus school of art and design.
5. Ferenc Erkel - a composer and conductor who is regarded as the father of Hungarian grand opera. He composed the music for the Hungarian national anthem.
6. Mihály Munkácsy - a painter who is considered one of the greatest Hungarian artists of all time. His works often depicted scenes from Hungarian peasant life.
7. Gyula Illyés - a poet, writer, and translator who is known for his contributions to Hungarian literature and his involvement in the Hungarian resistance movement during World War II.
8. Zsigmond Móricz - a novelist, journalist, and playwright who is regarded as one of the most important Hungarian writers of

the 20th century. His works often dealt with the lives of Hungarian peasants.

9. Károly Kós - an architect and politician who is known for his work in the field of traditional Hungarian architecture and for his efforts to preserve Hungarian cultural heritage.

10. Zsuzsa Koncz - a singer and actress who was a prominent figure in the Hungarian music scene in the 1960s and 1970s. She is known for her work as a singer-songwriter and for her contributions to Hungarian popular music.

E. 10 Most Photogenic Places in Budapest

Budapest is a city of stunning beauty, with an abundance of picturesque places that offer perfect photo opportunities. Whether you're a professional photographer or just someone who loves capturing moments, Budapest has something for everyone. From historic landmarks to hidden streets and romantic bridges, here are the top ten most photogenic places in Budapest:

1. Fisherman's Bastion: This neo-Gothic terrace offers a breathtaking panoramic view of the city and the Danube River. Capture the stunning view of the Parliament Building and the Chain Bridge from one of the seven turrets.
2. Buda Castle: This UNESCO World Heritage Site is a must-see when in Budapest. The castle's grand architecture and charming courtyards offer a unique opportunity for some amazing photos.
3. Parliament Building: The largest building in Hungary is also one of the most photographed landmarks in the city. Take a photo from across the river, or capture the grandeur of the building up close.
4. Széchenyi Chain Bridge: This iconic bridge is not only a symbol of Budapest but also a great spot for some beautiful photos, especially during the night when the city lights create a stunning reflection on the river.
5. St. Stephen's Basilica: This impressive basilica is not only a significant religious site but also a favorite spot for taking photos. Capture its grand dome or the intricate details of its interior.
6. Vajdahunyad Castle: This fairy-tale castle, located in the City Park, is a unique blend of different architectural styles. Take a photo of the castle's charming towers, bridges, and the surrounding lake.
7. Heroes' Square: This grand square features a towering column and statues of Hungary's most significant historical figures.

Capture the grandeur of the square, or take a close-up photo of the statues.

8. Danube Promenade: This scenic walkway along the Danube offers stunning views of the river and the city's landmarks. Capture the panoramic view of the city from one of the many vantage points along the promenade.

9. Gellért Hill: This elevated viewpoint offers a breathtaking view of the city, including the Parliament Building and the Danube River. Take a photo of the city from the Liberty Statue viewpoint or the Citadel.

10. Ruin Bars: Budapest's unique ruin bars are perfect for some artsy and hipster shots. The eclectic decor, colorful graffiti, and vintage atmosphere of these bars make for some great photo opportunities.

F. Local Events and Festivals

Budapest is a city that is alive with events and festivals throughout the year. The Hungarian capital is known for its music, art, and cultural events that attract visitors from all over the world. The city offers a range of activities and events, from international music festivals to traditional cultural events. Here are the top 10 most important local events and festivals in Budapest:

1. Budapest Wine Festival - held every September, the Budapest Wine Festival is one of the most popular events in the city. Visitors can sample a variety of wines from Hungary's best wineries, and enjoy live music and traditional Hungarian food.
2. Budapest International Documentary Festival - held annually in January, the Budapest International Documentary Festival showcases the best documentary films from around the world.
3. Budapest International Book Festival - held every April, the Budapest International Book Festival is the largest book event in Hungary, featuring book signings, lectures, and discussions with local and international authors.
4. Budapest Pride - the largest LGBTQ+ event in Hungary, Budapest Pride takes place in June and includes a variety of events, from parades to cultural events.
5. Budapest Summer Festival - held every summer, the Budapest Summer Festival includes a range of outdoor concerts, theater performances, and dance shows.
6. Budapest Design Week - held annually in October, Budapest Design Week celebrates the best of Hungarian design and includes exhibitions, workshops, and talks.
7. Budapest Christmas Fair - the Christmas Fair in Budapest is a festive event that takes place in the city's central Vörösmarty Square. Visitors can browse stalls selling traditional Hungarian gifts, food, and drink.
8. Budapest Fringe Festival - held every summer, the Budapest Fringe Festival showcases local and international performers, including theater, dance, and music.

9. Sziget Festival - one of the largest music festivals in Europe, Sziget Festival takes place every August and features a lineup of international musicians, as well as local artists.
10. Budapest Art Week - held annually in April, Budapest Art Week is a city-wide event that celebrates contemporary art with exhibitions, gallery openings, and talks.

II. Best Time to Visit Budapest

Budapest can be a great destination to visit at any time of year, depending on your preferences and interests. Here's an analysis of the best time to visit Budapest:

A. Weather Overview

The weather in Budapest can be quite variable, with hot summers and cold winters. The best time to visit Budapest for comfortable weather is during the shoulder seasons of spring (April to June) and autumn (September to November). During these times, temperatures are mild and there's less chance of rain or extreme weather. Summer (June to August) can be hot and humid, with occasional thunderstorms. Winter (December to February) can be cold, with occasional snow and icy conditions.

B. Peak Tourist Season

The peak tourist season in Budapest is during the summer months of June to August, when the weather is warm and there are many festivals and events happening in the city. This time of year can be quite busy and crowded, with higher prices for accommodations and attractions. It's important to book your accommodation and tickets in advance if you're planning to visit Budapest during this time.

C. Off-Season Travel

Off-season travel to Budapest can be a great option for budget-conscious travelers, as well as those who prefer quieter and less crowded destinations. The winter months of December to February can be especially charming, with Christmas markets, ice skating rinks, and other winter festivities. The shoulder seasons of spring and autumn can also be great times to visit, with milder weather, lower prices, and fewer crowds.

In general, the best time to visit Budapest depends on your preferences and interests. If you're interested in festivals, events, and outdoor activities, then the summer months may be the best choice for you. If you prefer milder weather and fewer crowds, then the shoulder seasons may be the best choice. And if you're on a tight budget or want to experience the city during a unique time of year, then off-season travel may be the best option for you.

III. Getting to and Around Budapest

Getting to and around Budapest can be easy and affordable, thanks to a range of transportation options that cater to all budgets and preferences. In this section, we'll take a closer look at the best ways to get to Budapest, as well as the most convenient ways to get around the city.

A. Airports and Transfers

Budapest has one major airport, the Budapest Ferenc Liszt International Airport (BUD), which is located approximately 16 kilometers (10 miles) southeast of the city center. Here's what you need to know about getting to and from the airport:

1. Public Transportation: The most convenient and affordable way to get to and from the airport is by using public transportation. The bus number 100E is a direct service from the airport to Deák Ferenc tér, a central location in Budapest. The trip takes about 35 minutes and costs 900 HUF (around 3 EUR) one way. Alternatively, you can take bus number 200E to Kőbánya-Kispest metro station and transfer to the metro line M3, which goes directly to the city center.

2. Taxi: Taxis are also available at the airport, and can be a convenient option if you have a lot of luggage or prefer a more direct route. The taxis have a fixed rate of 8000 HUF (around 25 EUR) to the city center, and you can find the taxi rank just outside the arrivals hall.

3. Private Transfer: Another option is to book a private transfer in advance. This can be a convenient option if you have a larger group or want to avoid waiting in line for public transportation or taxis. Private transfers can be arranged through various companies, and prices vary depending on the size of the group and the type of vehicle.

4. Useful Tips: When taking public transportation, it's important to purchase a ticket before boarding. You can buy tickets at the airport from the BKK desks, newsagents or vending

machines. It's also important to be aware of taxi scams, and to only use licensed taxis with a yellow registration plate.

By using one of these transportation options, you'll be able to reach the city center quickly and easily. No matter which option you choose, it's important to be aware of your surroundings and take necessary precautions to ensure a safe and hassle-free journey.

B. Public Transportation in Budapest

Budapest has a well-developed public transportation system that is affordable and convenient for getting around the city. The system includes metro, tram, bus, and trolleybus lines, all of which are interconnected and easy to navigate. Here's what you need to know about public transportation in Budapest:

1. Tickets and Passes: The easiest and most affordable way to use public transportation in Budapest is to purchase a ticket or pass. You can buy single tickets or discounted passes at vending machines located at most metro stations, newsstands, or customer service centers. It's important to validate your ticket or pass before boarding, as there are frequent ticket checks by the inspectors.

2. Types of Transportation: Budapest has three metro lines (M1, M2, M3), which run through the city center and to the suburbs. Trams and buses run throughout the city, and trolleybuses serve some of the major routes. Night buses and trams are also available.

3. Timetables and Route Planning: To plan your journey on public transportation, you can use the BKK website, which provides timetables, route planners, and up-to-date information on delays and disruptions. You can also download the BKK Futar app, which provides real-time information on the location and arrival times of buses, trams, and metro trains.

4. Travel Cards and Passes: For frequent travelers, it may be more cost-effective to purchase a travel card or pass. The Budapest Card, for example, provides unlimited use of public transportation, as well as free admission to some museums and discounts on other attractions. Other travel cards and passes are available for various lengths of time and for different zones.

Useful Tips: Be aware that public transportation in Budapest can be crowded during rush hour and on weekends, especially on popular routes. It's also important to keep an eye on your belongings and be aware of pickpockets, especially on crowded vehicles.

By using public transportation in Budapest, you'll be able to explore the city at your own pace, while saving money and avoiding traffic. It's a convenient and efficient way to get around, and with the right information and preparation, you can make the most of your experience.

C. Taxis and Ride-Sharing

Taxis and ridesharing services are available throughout Budapest and can be a convenient option for getting around the city. Here's what you need to know about taxis and ridesharing in Budapest:

1. Taxis: Taxis in Budapest are generally reliable and safe, but it's important to be aware of taxi scams, such as drivers overcharging tourists or taking unnecessarily long routes. To avoid these scams, always use licensed taxis with a yellow registration plate, and make sure that the meter is turned on and working properly before the trip begins.

2. Ridesharing: Ridesharing services, such as Uber and Bolt, are also available in Budapest, and can be a convenient and affordable alternative to taxis. These services allow you to book a ride through a mobile app, and the fare is calculated based on the distance traveled. The app also allows you to see

the driver's details, track the driver's location, and rate the driver after the trip.

3. Mobile Apps: To call taxis or book ridesharing services in Budapest, we recommend using the following mobile apps:
- Bolt: This ridesharing service is popular in Budapest, with competitive prices and a user-friendly app. You can book a ride in advance or in real-time, and the app also allows you to see the driver's rating and car details.
- Főtaxi: This is one of the largest taxi companies in Budapest, with a fleet of over 500 vehicles. You can book a taxi through the mobile app or by phone, and the app also allows you to track the driver's location and rate the driver after the trip.
- Taxify: This is another popular ridesharing service in Budapest, with affordable prices and a reliable service. You can book a ride through the app, and the app also allows you to see the driver's details and rate the driver after the trip.

By using these mobile apps, you'll be able to call taxis or book ridesharing services in Budapest easily and safely. Just be sure to check the prices and ratings before you book, and always use a licensed and trustworthy service.

D. More information

There are several transportation options available for getting to the city center, depending on your budget. For budget-friendly solutions, we recommend taking either the bus or the metro. Line 200 or 200E is the operating bus to look for. Here are the available options to get to the city center from Budapest Airport:

Taxi: Only use the yellow cabs! A taxi ride will cost between 4000-7000HUF and will take approximately 25 minutes to reach your accommodation.

Public transportation: This is the easiest and most affordable way to get to Budapest city center. Just follow the directions displayed in the arrivals terminal to quickly reach the bus. Purchase a standard ticket (350HUF) which will take you to the Kőbánya-Kispest stop. From there, hop on the Metro 3 (blue line) and ride for ten stops until you reach Deák Ferenc tér.

IV. Best Areas to Stay in Budapest

Budapest is a vibrant and exciting city, with plenty of neighborhoods and districts to choose from when looking for accommodations. In this section, we'll take a closer look at some of the best areas to stay in Budapest, based on their location, atmosphere, and attractions.

Whether you're looking for a luxury hotel in the heart of the city, a cozy apartment in a charming neighborhood, or a budget-friendly hostel with easy access to public transportation, we'll provide you with all the information you need to make the best choice for your trip. From the bustling nightlife of the Jewish Quarter to the elegant streets of the Castle District, Budapest has something for everyone.

By choosing the right area to stay in, you'll be able to immerse yourself in the local culture, explore the city's landmarks and attractions, and make the most of your time in Budapest. So, let's dive into the best areas to stay in Budapest and find the perfect accommodation for your trip!

A. District V: Inner City

District V, also known as the Inner City, is the heart of Budapest, and one of the most popular areas to stay for tourists. Here are some of the pros and cons of staying in this area:

Pros:

- Centrally located, with easy access to major attractions and public transportation
- Vibrant atmosphere, with many restaurants, cafes, and shops
- Beautiful architecture, including the Hungarian Parliament Building and St. Stephen's Basilica
- Safe and well-lit streets, with a low crime rate

Cons:

- Higher prices for accommodation and dining
- Crowded during peak tourist season

Top things to see and do in District V:

23

- Visit the Hungarian Parliament Building, one of the most iconic landmarks of Budapest
- Admire the stunning architecture of St. Stephen's Basilica and take a panoramic view of the city from the top of the dome
- Walk along the Danube Promenade and enjoy the beautiful view of the Buda Castle and the Chain Bridge
- Stroll through Vörösmarty Square, home to the famous Gerbeaud Café and a popular meeting spot for locals and tourists alike
- Explore the shops and restaurants of the lively Váci Street, the main pedestrian shopping street in Budapest

Accommodation options:
- Luxury: Aria Hotel Budapest by Library Hotel Collection - This 5-star hotel offers luxurious rooms with unique musical themes, a rooftop bar, a spa, and a central location.
- Mid-range: Hotel Parlament - This 4-star hotel offers modern and spacious rooms, a fitness center, and a great location close to the Parliament Building.
- Budget: Maverick City Lodge - This hostel offers affordable dorms and private rooms, a communal kitchen, and a prime location in the heart of the city.

No matter your budget or travel style, District V is a great area to stay in Budapest. With its central location, vibrant atmosphere, and beautiful landmarks, it's a perfect place to base yourself for exploring the city.

B. District VI: Terézváros
District VI, also known as Terézváros, is a lively and diverse neighborhood located just west of the Inner City. Here are some of the pros and cons of staying in this area:
Pros:
- Centrally located, with easy access to major attractions and public transportation

- Vibrant and trendy atmosphere, with many restaurants, bars, and cafes
- Great shopping, including the famous Andrássy Avenue and the WestEnd City Center mall
- Beautiful architecture, including the neo-Renaissance Opera House and the Art Nouveau buildings of Nagymező Street

Cons:
- Can be crowded and noisy, especially during peak tourist season
- Higher prices for accommodation and dining compared to other areas of Budapest

Top things to see and do in District VI:
- Attend a performance at the Hungarian State Opera House, one of the most beautiful opera houses in the world
- Walk along the elegant Andrássy Avenue, a UNESCO World Heritage Site lined with beautiful mansions, shops, and restaurants
- Visit the House of Terror Museum, a museum dedicated to the victims of the fascist and communist regimes in Hungary
- Explore the trendy Liszt Ferenc Square, a popular spot for dining and nightlife
- Relax in the City Park, home to the famous Széchenyi Thermal Bath and the Vajdahunyad Castle

Accommodation options:
- Luxury: Boscolo Budapest, Autograph Collection - This 5-star hotel offers luxurious rooms with beautiful decor, a spa, and a central location close to the Opera House.
- Mid-range: Hotel Medosz - This 3-star hotel offers comfortable and affordable rooms, a central location, and easy access to public transportation.
- Budget: Avenue Hostel - This hostel offers budget-friendly dorms and private rooms, a communal kitchen, and a great location close to the Opera House and Andrássy Avenue.

No matter your budget or travel style, District VI is a great area to stay in Budapest. With its central location, trendy atmosphere, and beautiful landmarks, it's a perfect place to base yourself for exploring the city.

C. District VII: Erzsébetváros

District VII, also known as Erzsébetváros, is a vibrant and eclectic neighborhood located just east of the Inner City. Here are some of the pros and cons of staying in this area:

Pros:
- Trendy and artistic atmosphere, with many galleries, cafes, and bars
- Affordable dining and accommodation options
- Convenient location, with easy access to public transportation
- Home to the famous ruin bars, a unique nightlife experience in Budapest

Cons:
- Can be noisy and crowded, especially during peak tourist season
- Some areas can be less safe at night

Top things to see and do in District VII:
- Explore the famous ruin bars, including Szimpla Kert and Instant, which offer a unique nightlife experience in Budapest
- Visit the Great Synagogue, the largest synagogue in Europe and a symbol of the Jewish community in Budapest
- Walk along Rumbach Sebestyén Street, a beautiful and historic street lined with ornate buildings
- Shop for vintage and retro finds at the boutiques and shops along Kazinczy Street
- Sample local street food and artisanal products at the Gozsdu Udvar, a popular food and drink destination

Accommodation options:
- Luxury: Hotel Moments Budapest - This 4-star hotel offers elegant rooms, a spa, and a great location close to the Inner City and the Great Synagogue.
- Mid-range: Hotel Gozsdu Court - This 3-star hotel offers modern and spacious rooms, a central location, and easy access to the Gozsdu Udvar.
- Budget: Wombats City Hostel Budapest - This hostel offers budget-friendly dorms and private rooms, a communal kitchen, and a great location close to the ruin bars.

No matter your budget or travel style, District VII is a great area to stay in Budapest. With its artistic atmosphere, affordable options, and unique landmarks, it's a perfect place to base yourself for exploring the city, especially if you're looking for a vibrant nightlife scene.

D.Where to Stay in Budapest: Our Top Recommendation

We highly recommend staying at the 12 Révay Hotel ("12 Révay Hotel."
) during your visit to Budapest. This modern and comfortable hotel is located in the heart of the city, at Révay utca 12, Budapest 1065, Hungary. For inquiries, you can reach them at (0036) 1909 1212. The hotel has received an outstanding rating of 9.2 out of 10 on Booking.com, making it an excellent choice for your stay.

Expect to pay approximately 25000-50000 HUF, or 80 to 160 Euros per night for a double room, depending on the terrace connection. The hotel boasts clean and well-appointed rooms and is conveniently located near several of the city's top attractions. Having lived on the same street for a year, we can attest to the hotel's prime location and the charm of the surrounding area.

V. Day 1: Exploring Pest

On your first day in Budapest, we recommend exploring the vibrant and bustling area of Pest. From the stunning St. Stephen's Basilica and the iconic Hungarian Parliament Building to the elegant Andrassy Avenue and the relaxing City Park, there's plenty to see and do in this historic and lively part of the city. And in the evening, you can experience the unique nightlife of the Jewish Quarter's famous ruin bars. Here's your itinerary for a perfect day in Pest.

A. Morning: St. Stephen's Basilica and Parliament Building

Your morning will begin with a visit to two of Budapest's most iconic landmarks, the St. Stephen's Basilica and the Hungarian Parliament Building.

St. Stephen's Basilica is a stunning neoclassical church dedicated to Hungary's first king, St. Stephen. The basilica features beautiful stained glass windows, intricate mosaics, and a grand dome that offers panoramic views of the city. You can also see the mummified hand of St. Stephen, which is kept in a chapel inside the basilica.

From St. Stephen's Basilica, it's just a short walk to the Hungarian Parliament Building, one of the most iconic landmarks of Budapest. The Parliament Building is a stunning example of neo-Gothic architecture, with a symmetrical facade, a grand staircase, and ornate decorations. You can take a guided tour of the building, which includes the magnificent session hall, the central staircase, and the Hungarian Crown Jewels.

B. Afternoon: Andrassy Avenue and City Park

After visiting the landmarks of the morning, it's time to explore the elegant Andrassy Avenue and the relaxing City Park.

Andrassy Avenue is a UNESCO World Heritage Site and one of the most elegant boulevards in Budapest. Lined with beautiful mansions, theaters, shops, and restaurants, it's a great place for a leisurely stroll or a coffee break. You can also visit the Hungarian State Opera House, a beautiful neo-Renaissance building, and the House of Terror Museum, which commemorates the victims of the fascist and communist regimes in Hungary.

From Andrassy Avenue, you can take a short metro ride to the City Park, a large public park that offers plenty of activities and attractions. The park is home to the famous Széchenyi Thermal Bath, the Vajdahunyad Castle, and the Museum of Fine Arts. You can also rent a bike, a rowboat, or a pedal boat, or just relax on the grass and enjoy the scenery.

C. Evening: Ruin Bars in the Jewish Quarter

In the evening, it's time to experience the unique nightlife of Budapest's Jewish Quarter, famous for its ruin bars. These bars are located in abandoned buildings, courtyards, and alleyways, and offer a unique and alternative atmosphere. Some of the most popular ruin bars include Szimpla Kert, Instant, and Fogas Ház.

In addition to the bars, the Jewish Quarter is also a great place to explore the local street art, vintage shops, and artisanal food and drink venues. You can also visit the Great Synagogue, the largest synagogue in Europe and a symbol of the Jewish community in Budapest.

By the end of the day, you'll have explored some of the most iconic landmarks and vibrant neighborhoods in Budapest. You'll also have experienced the unique and alternative nightlife of the Jewish Quarter. Enjoy a good night's rest, because Day 2 will be even more exciting!

VI. Day 2: Buda Castle and the Danube River

On your second day in Budapest, we recommend exploring the historic Buda Castle and the stunning Danube River. From the iconic Fisherman's Bastion and the elegant Buda Castle to the panoramic views from Gellert Hill and a scenic Danube River cruise, there's plenty to see and do in this beautiful part of the city. Here's your itinerary for a perfect day in Buda and the Danube River.

A. Morning: Buda Castle and Fisherman's Bastion

Your morning will begin with a visit to the Buda Castle and Fisherman's Bastion, two of the most iconic landmarks in Budapest.

Buda Castle is a beautiful complex of buildings, courtyards, and gardens located on a hill overlooking the Danube River. The castle was built in the 13th century and has been expanded and renovated over the centuries. You can visit the Royal Palace, the Matthias Church, and the Fisherman's Bastion, which offers stunning views of the city and the river.

Fisherman's Bastion is a neo-Gothic and neo-Romanesque terrace located on the Buda Castle Hill. It was built in the early 20th century and offers a panoramic view of the Danube River and the Pest side of the city. The terrace is named after the medieval fisherman's guild, who were responsible for defending this part of the city in the past.

B. Afternoon: Gellert Hill and the Citadella

After visiting the landmarks of the morning, it's time to enjoy the panoramic views from Gellert Hill and the Citadella.

Gellert Hill is a 235-meter-high hill located on the Buda side of the Danube River. It offers breathtaking views of the city and the river, as well as a beautiful park and a historic monument. You can also visit the Gellert Hill Cave, a natural cave that has been turned into a chapel.

At the top of Gellert Hill, you'll find the Citadella, a fortress built in the 19th century by the Habsburg Empire to control the city. Today, it offers stunning panoramic views of Budapest, and a great place to take photos and admire the beauty of the city.

C. Evening: Danube River Cruise and Dinner

In the evening, it's time to enjoy a scenic Danube River cruise and dinner, the perfect way to end your day in Budapest.

You can choose from a variety of river cruise options, from traditional sightseeing cruises to romantic dinner cruises. During the cruise, you'll see the famous landmarks of Budapest from a different perspective, including the Hungarian Parliament Building, the Buda Castle, and the Chain Bridge. You'll also enjoy a delicious dinner and drinks, while listening to live music and enjoying the beautiful views of the city.

By the end of the day, you'll have explored some of the most iconic landmarks and beautiful views in Budapest. You'll also have experienced the stunning Danube River from a different perspective. Enjoy a good night's rest, because Day 3 will be just as exciting!

VII. Day 3: Thermal Baths and Beyond

On your third day in Budapest, we recommend exploring the city's famous thermal baths and beautiful green spaces. From the relaxing Széchenyi Thermal Bath and the peaceful Margaret Island to the historic Heroes' Square and the delicious Hungarian cuisine, there's plenty to see and do in this beautiful part of the city. Here's your itinerary for a perfect day in Budapest.

A. Morning: Széchenyi Thermal Bath

Your morning will begin with a visit to the Széchenyi Thermal Bath, one of the largest and most popular thermal baths in Europe.

Széchenyi Thermal Bath is located in the City Park and offers 18 pools, both indoor and outdoor, as well as saunas, steam rooms, and massage services. The water in the pools comes from natural thermal springs and is believed to have healing properties. You can also try the famous chess game, played by regulars in the outdoor pool.

B. Afternoon: Margaret Island and Heroes' Square

After your relaxing morning, it's time to explore the beautiful Margaret Island and the historic Heroes' Square.

Margaret Island is a beautiful green oasis located in the middle of the Danube River. It offers beautiful parks, gardens, and fountains, as well as a historic convent and a musical fountain show. You can rent a bike, a Segway, or a pedal car, or just stroll around and enjoy the beautiful scenery.

Heroes' Square is a historic square located at the end of the elegant Andrassy Avenue. It features a monumental statue complex representing the Seven Chieftains of the Magyars and other important figures of Hungarian history. You can also visit the Museum of Fine Arts and the Art Gallery of Budapest, which are located on either side of the square.

C. Evening: Hungarian Cuisine and Folk Dancing

In the evening, it's time to taste the delicious Hungarian cuisine and experience the traditional folk dancing.

You can choose from a variety of restaurants and cafes offering authentic Hungarian dishes, such as goulash, paprika chicken, and chimney cake. You can also taste local wines and spirits, such as Tokaji wine and pálinka, a traditional fruit brandy.

After dinner, you can enjoy a traditional Hungarian folk dancing performance, which showcases the country's rich cultural heritage. Some of the most popular folk dance groups include the Hungarian State Folk Ensemble and the Rajkó Folk Ensemble.

By the end of the day, you'll have experienced the relaxing and healing properties of the thermal baths, the beauty of the city's green spaces, and the delicious flavors of the Hungarian cuisine. You'll also have experienced the unique and beautiful folk dancing of Hungary.

VIII. A General Purpose Hour-by-Hour 3 Days Itinerary

If you're short on time or prefer to follow a pre-planned itinerary, we've created a 3-day hour by hour itinerary that covers the most iconic landmarks and experiences in Budapest. This itinerary includes a detailed schedule for each day, including morning, afternoon, and evening activities, as well as estimated travel times and links to Google Maps for easy navigation. Whether you're a first-time visitor or a seasoned traveler, this itinerary is a great way to make the most of your time in Budapest and see the best that the city has to offer. So, pack your bags, put on your walking shoes, and get ready to explore the beautiful city of Budapest!

09:45 – Arrival at Liszt Ferenc Airport

Arrival at the Liszt Ferenc International Airport, **which is located 16km east-southeast of the city center.**

Budapest Liszt Ferenc International Airport is the largest airport in Hungary and serves as a hub for several airlines. Located approximately 16 kilometers from the city center, the airport offers a variety of transportation options for getting to and from the airport.

One of the most popular and budget-friendly options is to take public transportation. The airport is easily accessible by bus, with multiple routes available to the city center. The operating buses to look for are line 200E and 100E. Line 200E takes you to Kőbánya-Kispest metro station, where you can then take the M3 metro line to reach the city center. The cost of a single ticket is 350 HUF, and the journey takes approximately 45-60 minutes. Line 100E is a direct bus service to the city center and operates from Terminal 2. A single ticket for this bus costs 900 HUF, and the journey takes around 35-40 minutes.

Another option is to take a taxi, which is widely available outside the airport terminals. The ride to the city center takes about 25 minutes and costs approximately 4000-7000 HUF, depending on the destination.

Lastly, if you prefer a more comfortable and hassle-free experience, you can book a private transfer in advance. Several companies offer this service, and prices vary depending on the type of vehicle and the number of passengers.

09:55 – Passport Control

Take the luggage and pass through passport control.

If you're traveling with only carry-on luggage, it typically takes just 3 to 5 minutes to pass through the baggage claim area and exit to the arrivals terminal.

10:05 – Head to the Hotel

There are several options for reaching 12 Révay Hotel from the airport. If you prefer public transportation, you can take either the bus or shuttle after using the metro. A standard ticket for the bus costs 3500 HUF or 1.2 Euros, and the journey takes approximately 25 minutes. The recommended stop to get off at is Kőbánya-Kispest. Alternatively, taking the metro (Blue line, number 3) is also an affordable option, costing the same amount and taking 15 minutes. The recommended stop to get off at is Deák Ferenc tér.

If you prefer a more direct route, a taxi ride is also an option. The journey takes approximately 25 minutes and costs between 4000-7000 HUF or 13 to 25 euros, depending on the taxi service and traffic conditions.

11:20 – Bazilika, Deak Ferenc Square

After checking into your hotel, you can explore the city's top monuments on foot. Take some time to refresh yourself at the hotel before embarking on your adventure. Many of Budapest's most famous landmarks are easily accessible by foot, making it a convenient way to see the sights.

View ZoomTip 1.2, costs: **Bazilika:** free entrance, panoramic view 500HUF/person, **Deák Ferenc Square:** Free

14:00 – Lunch at Borkonyha

Enjoy your midday meal at Borkonyha Restaurant, located at Sas utca 3 in Budapest (zip code 1051), with a contact phone number of (0036) 1 266 0835. This unique establishment offers a fusion of a French bistro, a Hungarian family restaurant, and a wine shop and bar. With over 200 types of wines, mostly from small and large Hungarian wineries, Borkonyha is a great place to indulge in the local wine culture. It's no surprise that the restaurant was awarded a Michelin star in 2014.

*View *ZoomTip 1.3,* Main course Costs around 3500-5000 HUF (15 to 20 euros).

15:30 - Visit the Market at Fővám tér
(Budapest's famous traditional market, with lots of meat, vegetables, and fruits)

*View *ZoomTip 1.4,* Ticket Price: Free

18:00 – Vaci Street
Stroll down Váci Street, known as one of the busiest and most commercialized areas in Budapest. However, since it's often crowded with both locals and tourists, be mindful of potential pickpockets. Take a moment to unwind at one of the many charming cafes that line this beautiful avenue.

*View *ZoomTip 1.5*

20:00 – Dinner at Belgrad
For dinner, head to the Belgrád rakpart area where you can find a plethora of excellent restaurants. The best part is that you'll get to enjoy stunning views of the Danube River as a bonus.

*View *ZoomTip 1.6,* cost: 5000HUF per person.

22:00 – Back at the Hotel
Walk back to your hotel and rest.

1st Day in Budapest Map

To help you navigate the first day of your Budapest adventure, we've created a detailed Google Map that includes all the locations mentioned in the morning, afternoon, and evening itinerary. This map is designed to make it easy for you to find your way around the city and explore each location without any hassle. To use the map, simply open the link we've provided and follow the itinerary, starting with St. Stephen's Basilica and Parliament Building in the morning, then moving on to Andrassy Avenue and City Park in the afternoon, and finally the Jewish Quarter's Ruin Bars in the evening.

Each location on the map is marked with a pin and includes a brief description of the attraction or landmark. You can click on the pins to see more details, such as opening hours, admission fees, and other useful information. You can also use the "directions" feature to get step-by-step directions from your current location to the attraction.

We hope that this map will help you make the most of your time in Budapest and make your first day a fun and easy experience. Enjoy your trip, and happy exploring!

Budapest 1st Day Map: Get it Online By Clicking Here

Bazilika

St. Stephen's Basilica, also known as Bazilika, is a stunning neoclassical church in Budapest and one of the most iconic landmarks of the city. Here are some tips, visitor information, and interesting facts about the Bazilika:

Tips:

- To avoid the crowds, visit the basilica early in the morning or late in the afternoon.
- Dress appropriately, as the basilica is a religious site. Shorts, sleeveless tops, and short skirts are not allowed.
- Be respectful of the religious services that take place in the basilica, especially during mass or other ceremonies.

Visitor information:
- The basilica is open every day from 9:00 am to 7:00 pm, with extended hours on weekends and holidays.
- Admission to the basilica is free, but there is a fee for visiting the observation deck of the dome or for taking the guided tour.
- The dress code for the basilica requires modest clothing that covers the shoulders and knees.

What to notice:
- The basilica's grand dome, which is one of the tallest structures in Budapest and offers stunning panoramic views of the city.
- The beautiful stained glass windows and intricate mosaics that adorn the walls and ceilings of the basilica.
- The mummified hand of St. Stephen, which is kept in a chapel inside the basilica and is a popular attraction for visitors.

Interesting facts:
- St. Stephen's Basilica is named after Hungary's first king, St. Stephen, who is also the patron saint of the country.
- The basilica was built in the late 19th century, after several earlier attempts to build a grand church on the site were unsuccessful due to wars and financial difficulties.
- The basilica's dome was inspired by the dome of the Pantheon in Rome, and its height was intentionally designed to be one meter taller than that of the nearby Hungarian Parliament Building.

Overall, St. Stephen's Basilica is a must-see attraction in Budapest and a great example of the city's rich cultural and architectural heritage. Whether you're interested in the stunning artwork and architecture of the basilica, the religious and cultural significance of the site, or just the panoramic views from the dome, a visit to the Bazilika is an essential part of any Budapest itinerary.

Hours: 9.00am – 5.00pm
Ticket Price: panoramic view 500HUF

ZoomTip 1.3: Borkonyha

Borkonyha, which translates to "Wine Kitchen" in English, is a Michelin-starred restaurant in Budapest that offers an exceptional culinary experience, focusing on the flavors of Hungarian cuisine and the best Hungarian wines. Here's what you need to know about Borkonyha and some of the suggested dishes to try:

Atmosphere: Borkonyha's atmosphere is elegant and sophisticated, with a sleek and modern design that emphasizes the beauty of the historic building in which the restaurant is located. The ambiance is refined yet welcoming, with an emphasis on the quality of the food and wine.

Menu: Borkonyha's menu is a celebration of the best Hungarian ingredients and flavors, with an emphasis on modern interpretations of traditional dishes. The menu changes frequently to reflect the availability of seasonal ingredients, and the wine list is extensive, with a focus on Hungarian wines.

Suggested dishes:

- Duck liver terrine with pickled beetroot and walnut bread
- Sea bass with Jerusalem artichoke purée, crispy onion, and red wine sauce
- Pork belly with roasted parsnip, quince, and port wine jus
- Beef tenderloin with horseradish cream, roasted garlic, and red wine sauce
- Poppy seed cake with caramelized white chocolate mousse and plum sorbet

The quality of the food, the creativity of the presentation, and the attention to detail in each dish are all exceptional at Borkonyha. The

staff is knowledgeable and friendly, and they are happy to recommend wine pairings to enhance the flavors of each dish.
If you're looking for a special and unforgettable dining experience in Budapest, Borkonyha is definitely worth a visit.

Address: 1051 Budapest, Sas utca 3.
Telephone: 0036 1 266 0835

ZoomTip 1.4: Fővám tér market

Fővám tér market, also known as the Central Market Hall, is one of the most iconic landmarks of Budapest and a popular destination for both locals and tourists. Here's what you need to know about Fővám tér market:

History
The market was built in the late 19th century and was designed by the famous Hungarian architect Samu Pecz. It was originally intended to be a modern and hygienic space for selling fresh produce and meat, and it quickly became a hub for local commerce and social life. Atmosphere: The market's architecture is stunning, with a wrought-iron structure and a colorful, tiled roof that creates a bright and welcoming space. The atmosphere is lively and bustling, with vendors selling a variety of goods, from fresh produce and meats to spices, souvenirs, and handmade crafts. The market is a great place to experience the local culture and get a taste of the authentic flavors of Hungary.

Shopping

The market is divided into three floors. On the ground floor, you'll find a variety of vendors selling fresh produce, meats, cheeses, and breads. You can also find traditional Hungarian snacks, such as lángos (deep-fried dough topped with cheese and sour cream) and kürtőskalács (chimney cake), which are popular among locals and tourists alike.

The first floor is dedicated to souvenirs, clothing, and other tourist items, and the second floor houses the food court, which offers a variety of traditional Hungarian dishes, such as goulash, stuffed cabbage, and chimney cake.

Tips

The market is open every day from 6:00 am to 6:00 pm, except for Sundays and public holidays.
The best time to visit the market is in the morning when the vendors are setting up their stalls and the produce is at its freshest.
Be aware of pickpockets and keep your belongings close to you, especially in crowded areas.

Visiting Fővám tér market is a great way to experience the local culture and taste the flavors of Hungarian cuisine. Whether you're shopping for fresh produce, trying traditional snacks, or exploring the stalls for unique souvenirs, the market is a must-see destination in Budapest.

Address: 1093 Budapest, Vámház körút 1-3.
Telephone: 0036 1 366 3300

ZoomTip 1.5: Váci Street

Váci Street is the most famous pedestrian shopping street in Budapest. It stretches to a little more than a mile between Vörösmarty Square and the Great Market Hall.

Váci Street is one of the most famous and vibrant streets in Budapest, and a popular destination for locals and tourists alike. Here's what you need to know about Váci Street, its history, and the best things to notice:

History: Váci Street has a rich and fascinating history that dates back to the medieval times. Originally, it was a small street in the old town of Buda, and was primarily used as a trading route for merchants and craftsmen. Over time, the street grew in size and popularity, and it became a hub for commerce and social life in the city.

In the 19th century, Váci Street underwent a major transformation, and many of the old buildings were replaced with new and modern structures. During this time, it became known as the "Champs-Elysées of Budapest" and was a popular destination for the city's elite.

Today, Váci Street is one of the most iconic and bustling streets in Budapest, with a wide variety of shops, restaurants, and cafes.

Best things to notice:
- The architecture: Váci Street is lined with beautiful and historic buildings, many of which have been restored to their former glory. The facades of the buildings feature a variety of architectural styles, including Baroque, Art Nouveau, and Renaissance.
- The shopping: Váci Street is a shopper's paradise, with a wide variety of shops offering everything from high-end fashion to handmade crafts and souvenirs. Some of the most popular shops include Zara, H&M, and Swarovski.
- The cafes and restaurants: Váci Street is home to a wide variety of cafes and restaurants, offering everything from traditional Hungarian cuisine to international fare. Some of the most popular options include the traditional Hungarian restaurant, Café Vian, and the elegant Gerlóczy Café.
- The street performers: Váci Street is always buzzing with activity, and you'll often find street performers entertaining passersby with music, dance, and other performances.

Tips:
- Váci Street can get very crowded, especially during the peak tourist season. Try to visit during the morning or late evening to avoid the crowds.
- Keep an eye out for pickpockets, especially in crowded areas.
- Take the time to explore the side streets and alleys off of Váci Street, as they often offer hidden gems and unique experiences.

Overall, Váci Street is a must-see destination in Budapest, offering a unique blend of history, culture, and modern life. Whether you're shopping, dining, or just taking in the sights and sounds of the street, Váci Street is a vibrant and unforgettable experience.

Day 2: Danube River tour

09:30 - Bridge cruise over the Danube

Experience the best that Budapest has to offer with a river cruise. You can purchase your ticket at many of the tourist points located in the city center, or book online at http://www.budapestdanubecruise.com/.

During the daytime sightseeing cruise, you'll be guided along the river by the two parts of the town, Buda and Pest, as they share the fascinating stories behind the city's iconic sights. The cruise ends at Margaret Island, where you'll have the option to get off the ship and explore the island on foot. If you'd prefer not to visit the island, you can stay on board and enjoy the scenic ride back to the center. The ship makes a brief 5-minute stop before continuing its journey towards the city center.

Price: 3900HUF/person

11:45 - Visit the *Margaret Island*

Take a pleasant stroll along Margaret Island and enjoy a delicious lunch while you're there. We recommend trying the street food near the fountain, where you can savor the mouthwatering Hungarian sausages. Simply follow the enticing aroma to find them!

*View *ZoomTip 2.1*

13:45 - Visit the park of Vigadó

Once you've finished exploring the island, hop on the next boat back to the city center. We suggest making a stop at Vigadó tér, where you can take a leisurely stroll, or stop at Kiosk Bar for a delicious cup of coffee.

Address: Budapest, Március 15. Tér 4., 1056, View *ZoomTip 2.2*

Day 2: Budapest Parliament

16:00 - Visit the Parliament of Budapest

From Vigadó tér, just walk next to the Danube, and you can quickly reach the Parliament.

As the millennial celebrations of 1896 approached, the nation's demand for representation channeled the conception of a unique Parliament building. The Palace of Westminster in part inspired the design, but a well-known Hungarian architect, Imre Steindl, laid out the plans in their entirety. The building stretches 268 meters in its length, along with the Danube embankment.

*View *ZoomTip 2.3*

18:00 - Hero's square

Take a pleasant walk back to Deák Ferenc Square, and then hop on the Yellow Line (Metro line 1). Ride the metro until you reach Heroes Square (Hősök tere), one of the most prominent squares in Budapest. The square is famous for its iconic statue complex, which features the Seven Chieftains of the Magyars, along with other prominent national leaders. Don't miss the opportunity to visit the Tomb of the Unknown Soldier while you're there.

*View *ZoomTip 2.4*

20:00 - Dinner at Bagolyvár

Located near Hero's Square, this restaurant serves an array of delectable Hungarian specialties. While it may not be the most affordable option, we believe the experience is well worth it.

*Address: Budapest 1146 Gundel Károly út 4, Main course: 3000-6000HUF, View *ZoomTip 2.5*

22:00 - Relax at a bar: 360 Bar

360 Bar offers an exceptional rooftop experience with stunning views of Budapest. Relax after a long and exciting day exploring the city while sipping on lovely cocktails and listening to great music.

*Address: Andrássy út 39. Budapest, Hungary 1061 View *ZoomTip 2.6*

Budapest 2nd Day Map

Each location on the map is marked with a pin and includes a brief description of the attraction or landmark. You can click on the pins to see more details, such as opening hours, admission fees, and other useful information. You can also use the "directions" feature to get step-by-step directions from your current location to the attraction.

We hope that this map will help you make the most of your time in Budapest and make your second day a fun and easy experience. Enjoy your trip, and happy exploring!

Budapest 2nd Day Map: Get it Online By Clicking Here

ZoomTip 2.1: Margaret Island

Margaret Island

Margaret Island is a beautiful park located on an island in the middle of the Danube River, right in the heart of Budapest. It's a popular spot for locals and tourists alike, offering a peaceful retreat from the bustling city.

To reach the island, you can take the number 26 bus from Nyugati Railway Station, or tram number 4 or 6 from the city center. The cost is the same as a standard public transport ticket (350 HUF or around 1.2 EUR), and the journey takes about 10-15 minutes.

The island is steeped in history and has been a popular recreational spot for centuries. It was named after Princess Margaret, the daughter of King Béla IV, who was sent to the island for protection during the Mongol invasion in the 13th century. Over the years, the island has been used for various purposes, including as a royal garden, a hunting ground, and even as a Franciscan convent.

Today, Margaret Island is a sprawling park filled with lush greenery, walking and cycling paths, and beautiful gardens. There are also a number of attractions on the island, including the famous musical fountain, the Palatinus outdoor pool complex, and the Alfréd Hajós sports pool, which was built for the 1958 World Aquatics Championships.

Visitors can also enjoy a round of mini-golf, play a game of chess on the giant chessboard, or simply relax on one of the many benches and enjoy the peaceful surroundings. The island is also home to several restaurants and cafes, as well as a small zoo, and a Japanese garden.

Margaret Island is a popular destination for locals and tourists alike, offering a chance to escape the hustle and bustle of the city and connect with nature. With its rich history and diverse attractions, it's definitely worth a visit during your stay in Budapest.

Ticket Price: Free

ZoomTip 2.2: Vigado Ter

Vigadó tér is a beautiful public square located in the heart of Budapest, Hungary. The square is surrounded by some of the city's most impressive buildings, including the Vigadó Concert Hall, which is located at the center of the square.

The Vigadó Concert Hall is one of the oldest and most important concert halls in Budapest, and has been a popular venue for music and cultural events since the 19th century. The building was originally designed by Frigyes Feszl, and underwent extensive renovations in the early 2000s to restore it to its former glory. Today, the hall is a stunning example of neo-baroque architecture, and is known for its beautiful frescoes, intricate carvings, and elaborate chandeliers.

In addition to the concert hall, Vigadó tér is also home to several other notable buildings, including the Gresham Palace, which was designed by the famous Hungarian architect Zsigmond Quittner in the early

20th century. The Gresham Palace is now home to the Four Seasons Hotel, and is known for its Art Nouveau style and ornate decorations.

Visitors to Vigadó tér can also enjoy a leisurely stroll around the square, which is filled with beautiful trees, gardens, and fountains. There are also several cafes and restaurants located in the area, where you can enjoy a cup of coffee or a meal while taking in the sights and sounds of this historic part of Budapest.

Overall, Vigadó tér is a must-visit destination for anyone interested in architecture, history, and culture. Whether you're attending a concert at the Vigadó Concert Hall or simply taking in the beautiful surroundings, this square is sure to leave a lasting impression on you.

Ticket Price: Free

ZoomTip 2.3: Hungarian Parliament

Hungarian Parliament

The Hungarian Parliament is one of the most iconic buildings in Budapest and is one of the largest parliament buildings in the world. Located on the banks of the Danube River, the Parliament is a stunning example of neo-gothic architecture and is a must-see attraction for anyone visiting the city.

Built in the late 19th century, the Hungarian Parliament was designed by Hungarian architect Imre Steindl and took over 20 years to complete. The building features a central dome that reaches a height of 96 meters, and is adorned with intricate carvings, sculptures, and other decorative elements.

Visitors to the Hungarian Parliament can take guided tours of the building, which offer a fascinating insight into the history and politics of Hungary. One of the highlights of the tour is the opportunity to see the building's central hall, which features a stunning vaulted ceiling and is decorated with frescoes and mosaics.

Another notable feature of the Hungarian Parliament is the crown jewels, which are kept in a special room in the building. The crown jewels are a symbol of Hungary's rich history and are said to date back to the early days of the Hungarian monarchy.

One thing to notice while visiting the Hungarian Parliament is the impressive staircase that leads to the building's entrance. The staircase features a red carpet and is flanked by two imposing statues, which add to the grandeur of the building's exterior.

Overall, a visit to the Hungarian Parliament is a must-do activity for anyone visiting Budapest. Whether you're interested in architecture, history, or politics, the Parliament offers a fascinating glimpse into the culture and traditions of Hungary.

ZoomTip 2.4: Hero's Square

Hero's Square, or Hősök tere in Hungarian, is a major square located at the end of Andrássy Avenue in Budapest, Hungary. It is one of the city's most popular tourist attractions and is an important cultural landmark.

The square is dominated by a massive statue complex that pays tribute to Hungary's most important historical figures, including the Seven Chieftains of the Magyars and other prominent national leaders. The centerpiece of the complex is the Millennium Monument, which was erected in 1896 to celebrate the 1000th anniversary of the arrival of the Magyars in the Carpathian Basin.

In addition to the statue complex, Hero's Square is surrounded by several important cultural institutions, including the Museum of Fine Arts and the Palace of Art. The Museum of Fine Arts houses one of the largest collections of artwork in Hungary, including works by famous artists such as Raphael, Rembrandt, and Rubens.

Visitors to Hero's Square can also take a stroll around the City Park, which is located just behind the square. The park is one of the largest green spaces in Budapest and offers a wide range of recreational activities, including boating on the lake, ice skating in the winter, and exploring the beautiful gardens and walking paths.

Hero's Square is also a popular location for festivals and events throughout the year. In the summer months, the square hosts several cultural events, including concerts, dance performances, and traditional Hungarian festivals.

Overall, Hero's Square is a must-see attraction for anyone visiting Budapest. With its impressive statue complex, beautiful surrounding park, and cultural institutions, the square offers a fascinating glimpse into Hungary's rich history and vibrant cultural traditions.

ZoomTip 2.5: Bagolyvar Restaurant

Bagolyvár Restaurant

Bagolyvár Restaurant is a charming and elegant restaurant located in the heart of Buda, just a short walk from the Buda Castle. Here's what you need to know about Bagolyvár Restaurant:

Atmosphere: Bagolyvár Restaurant is housed in a beautifully restored 16th-century building, with a warm and inviting ambiance that reflects the rich history and culture of the area. The interior features a mix of traditional and contemporary design elements, with antique furnishings, rich fabrics, and warm lighting. The atmosphere is cozy and intimate, making it the perfect place for a romantic dinner or a special occasion.

Menu: Bagolyvár Restaurant offers a range of traditional Hungarian dishes, made from locally-sourced and seasonal ingredients. The menu includes a variety of appetizers, soups, main courses, and desserts, as well as an extensive wine list that features some of the best Hungarian wines. Some of the most popular dishes include the roasted duck breast with red cabbage and chestnut puree, the beef tenderloin with mushroom ragout and truffle sauce, and the traditional Hungarian goulash.

Service: The staff at Bagolyvár Restaurant are known for their warm and welcoming hospitality, and are happy to provide recommendations or help you choose the perfect wine to accompany your meal. The service is attentive and professional, without being overbearing, and the staff are knowledgeable about the menu and the history of the restaurant.

Price: Bagolyvár Restaurant is a higher-end dining option in Budapest, with prices that are commensurate with the quality of the food and the ambiance. While it is more expensive than some of the other restaurants in the area, it is still affordable compared to similar restaurants in other major cities.

Tips:
- Reservations are recommended, especially on weekends or during peak tourist season.
- Dress code is smart casual, so dress to impress.

Overall, Bagolyvár Restaurant is a great choice for anyone looking for a memorable dining experience in Budapest. The quality of the food, the warm ambiance, and the attentive service make it a must-visit destination for anyone looking to experience the best of Hungarian cuisine and culture.

ZoomTip 2.6:

360 Bar

360 Bar is a popular rooftop bar located in the heart of Budapest, and is known for its stunning panoramic views of the city. Here's what you need to know about 360 Bar:

Atmosphere:
360 Bar has a sleek and modern design, with a chic and sophisticated ambiance that is perfect for a night out with friends or a romantic evening. The bar features a spacious outdoor terrace with comfortable seating, a well-stocked bar, and live music or DJ performances on certain nights. The ambiance is both relaxing and energizing, with a lively atmosphere and stunning views of the city.

Drinks:
360 Bar offers a wide variety of drinks, including classic cocktails, craft beers, and an extensive selection of wines and champagnes. The bartenders are skilled and knowledgeable, and are happy to

recommend a drink based on your preferences or mood. The prices are reasonable for a rooftop bar of this quality, and there is a good variety of options to choose from.

Food:
360 Bar also offers a selection of small bites and snacks to accompany your drinks, such as cheese platters, charcuterie boards, and bruschetta. While the food menu is not extensive, the quality is good and the portions are perfect for sharing with a group of friends.

View:
The main attraction of 360 Bar is its panoramic views of the city, which are truly breathtaking. From the terrace, you can see the iconic landmarks of Budapest, including the Danube River, the Chain Bridge, the Parliament Building, and the Buda Castle. The views are especially stunning at sunset and at night, when the city is illuminated and glows with a magical light.

Tips:

- The bar can get very crowded, especially on weekends or during peak tourist season. Try to arrive early or make a reservation to ensure a table.
- Dress code is casual but trendy, so be sure to dress to impress.
- While the bar is open year-round, it is most enjoyable during the warmer months when you can sit outside and take in the views.

Overall, 360 Bar is a must-visit destination in Budapest, offering stunning views, great drinks, and a lively atmosphere. Whether you're looking for a romantic evening, a night out with friends, or just a relaxing drink after a day of sightseeing, 360 Bar is a perfect spot to experience the best of Budapest.

Day 3: Buda side of Budapest and Spa Day

09:00 - Visit the Buda Castle

Explore the historic castle district of Budapest by taking a tour of the Buda Castle and discovering the many attractions and hidden gems that are found on the Buda Castle Hill. Thanks to the excellent location of your hotel, you can even take a leisurely 20-minute walk to the Buda Castle, taking in the stunning scenery along the way.

*View *ZoomTip 3.1,* Tour Price: 9000HUF

11:00 - Visit the Mátyás Church

Just a short walk from the Buda Castle, you will find the grand Matthias Church. This stunning Roman Catholic church is located in Budapest, Hungary, and is situated in front of the Fisherman's Bastion at the heart of Buda's Castle District. According to church tradition, the building was initially constructed in Romanesque style in 1015, although no archaeological remains exist.

*View *ZoomTip 3.2,* Opening hours: 9 am – 5 pm,Ticket Price: 1400HUF

12:00 - Lunch break at Budavári Mátyás Restaurant

Time for another one of Budapest's best restaurant! Hungarian dishes

*View *ZoomTip 3.3,* Address: 1014 Budapest, Hess András tér 4, Website: http://www.budavarimatyasetterem.hu/, Main courses: 3000-5000HUF

14:00 - Halászbástya

Undoubtedly, Fisherman's Bastion in Budapest is one of the top attractions to visit. Take a stroll around the bastion to enjoy the magnificent panoramic views of Budapest.

*View *ZoomTip 3.4,* Ticket Price: free

15:00 - Széchenyi Spa

Take the bus number 16 to return to Deák Ferenc square, then transfer to Metro 1 (yellow line) and disembark at Mexikói út.

*View *ZoomTip 3.5,* Ticket Price: 5000HUF/person

20:30 - Dinner at Callas, just next to Opera House

Located in the heart of Budapest, you can enjoy your final Hungarian meal in the vicinity of the stunning Opera House.

*Address: Budapest, VI. kerület, Andrássy út 20., Main course: 3000-5000HUF, View *ZoomTip 3.6*

23:00 - Return to the Hotel

Get some rest, as you have an early flight to catch tomorrow..

Budapest 3d Day Map

Each location on the map is marked with a pin and includes a brief description of the attraction or landmark. You can click on the pins to see more details, such as opening hours, admission fees, and other useful information. You can also use the "directions" feature to get step-by-step directions from your current location to the attraction.

We hope that this map will help you make the most of your time in Budapest and make your second day a fun and easy experience. Enjoy your trip, and happy exploring!

Budapest 3d Day Map: Get it Online By Clicking Here

ZoomTip 3.1: Buda Castle

Buda Castle

History: Buda Castle, also known as the Royal Palace, is a massive palace complex located on the Buda side of the Danube River. It was originally built in the 13th century and has undergone many changes and renovations over the centuries. The castle was the official residence of the Hungarian kings for over 700 years, until it was heavily damaged during World War II. It has since been restored and now houses several museums, galleries, and government offices.

Things to See: Buda Castle is a massive complex with a wide variety of things to see and do. Here are some of the highlights:
- Hungarian National Gallery: This museum showcases Hungarian art from the Middle Ages to the present day, with a particular focus on 19th- and 20th-century artists.

- Budapest History Museum: This museum explores the history of Budapest, from its Roman roots to the present day, with a special emphasis on the medieval and Ottoman periods.
- Matthias Church: This stunning Gothic church is located at the heart of the castle complex and features intricate stonework, colorful stained glass windows, and a beautiful interior.
- Fisherman's Bastion: This ornate terrace offers stunning panoramic views of the city and the Danube River, and is a popular spot for taking photos.

Interesting Facts:
- Buda Castle is the largest castle complex in Hungary, spanning over 4 hectares.
- The castle was destroyed and rebuilt several times over the centuries, with the most recent major renovation taking place in the 20th century.
- The castle has been used as a filming location for several movies, including "The English Patient" and "Evita."

Visitor Information:
- The castle complex is open every day, although the opening hours vary depending on the specific attraction or museum. It's best to check the hours in advance.
- Admission fees also vary depending on the attraction or museum. Some offer discounted rates for students or seniors, and some may be free on certain days.
- It's possible to explore the castle complex on foot, but it's quite large, so wear comfortable shoes and be prepared to do some walking.
- There are several cafes and restaurants located within the castle complex, as well as souvenir shops and galleries.
- It's possible to reach the castle via the Castle Hill Funicular or by walking up the hill from the Danube River.

Overall, Buda Castle is a must-see destination in Budapest, with its stunning architecture, rich history, and wide variety of attractions and museums. Whether you're interested in art, history, or just want to take in the beautiful views of the city, Buda Castle is a perfect destination for any traveler visiting Budapest.

ZoomTip 3.2: Matthias Church

Matthias Church, also known as the Church of Our Lady, is a stunning Roman Catholic church located in the Castle District of Budapest. With its vibrant colors and intricate details, the Matthias Church is an excellent example of the late Gothic style of architecture. The church's origins can be traced back to the 13th century, but it has undergone several renovations and restorations over the centuries.

One of the most striking features of the Matthias Church is its stunning tile roof, which features an intricate pattern of green, yellow, and red tiles. The church's main entrance is also an architectural masterpiece, featuring a magnificent rose window and two beautifully crafted bell towers.

Inside the church, visitors can admire the breathtaking Gothic interior, which is decorated with stained glass windows, frescoes, and murals. The most notable artwork is the ornate altarpiece, which is considered a masterpiece of Renaissance art. Visitors can also see the tomb of King Béla III and his wife Anne, as well as the memorial plaques of several Hungarian national heroes.

To fully appreciate the Matthias Church, visitors should take note of the intricate details, such as the ornate stone carvings and the delicate wood carvings of the pulpit. The church's acoustics are also noteworthy, as it is often used as a venue for classical music concerts and organ recitals.

Overall, a visit to the Matthias Church is a must-see for anyone visiting Budapest. Its unique blend of Gothic and Renaissance architecture, stunning interior, and rich history make it one of the city's top attractions.

ZoomTip 3.3: **Budavári Mátyás Étterem**

Budavári Mátyás Étterem is a must-visit restaurant in Budapest for anyone interested in Hungarian cuisine. Located in the historic Castle District, the restaurant offers traditional Hungarian dishes and excellent service in a cozy and welcoming atmosphere.

One of the standout features of Budavári Mátyás Étterem is its menu, which features classic Hungarian dishes such as goulash, stuffed cabbage, and beef stroganoff, all prepared with high-quality ingredients and a focus on authenticity. There are also many vegetarian options, as well as international dishes and an extensive wine list.

The restaurant has both indoor and outdoor seating, with a charming terrace overlooking the surrounding cobblestone streets of the Castle

District. The staff is friendly and attentive, ensuring a pleasant dining experience.

When visiting Budavári Mátyás Étterem, it is recommended to make a reservation in advance, especially for dinner. The prices are higher than average, but the quality of the food and service is worth it.

One tip for visitors is to try the Hungarian wine, which pairs perfectly with the traditional dishes on the menu. The sommelier can help with recommendations based on your preferences.

Another tip is to arrive early to enjoy a drink on the terrace before dinner, and take a stroll around the picturesque streets of the Castle District.

Overall, Budavári Mátyás Étterem is an excellent choice for anyone looking to experience Hungarian cuisine in a cozy and historic setting, with quality food and attentive service.

ZoomTip 3.4: Halászbástya

Halászbástya, also known as the Fisherman's Bastion, is a beautiful monument located in Budapest's Castle District. This stunning bastion offers some of the best panoramic views of Budapest, making it a must-visit attraction for any tourist.

Built in the early 20th century, the Fisherman's Bastion is a neo-Gothic and neo-Romanesque architectural masterpiece that consists of seven towers that symbolize the seven Hungarian tribes that founded the country. The structure also features numerous staircases, walking paths, and terraces that offer stunning views of the Danube River, Pest, and the surrounding hills.

The name "Fisherman's Bastion" is derived from the medieval fishermen's guild, which was responsible for defending this part of the city during the Middle Ages. The bastion's design is heavily influenced by the romantic style of the Middle Ages, and the walls are adorned with beautiful stone carvings and intricate details.

Today, the Fisherman's Bastion is a popular tourist destination, and it offers a unique and romantic atmosphere for visitors to enjoy. One of the highlights of the bastion is the Matthias Church, which is located adjacent to the monument. The church is an impressive Gothic structure that features beautiful stained glass windows, a breathtaking altar, and impressive frescoes.

Visitors to the Fisherman's Bastion can enjoy exploring the complex, taking in the stunning views, and taking photographs. There are also numerous souvenir shops and cafes located within the complex, making it a great place to relax and enjoy a cup of coffee or tea while taking in the views.

If you're planning to visit the Fisherman's Bastion, it's important to note that there is a small admission fee to enter the upper terraces. However, the lower terraces are free to access, and they offer equally stunning views of the city. It's also worth noting that the Fisherman's Bastion can get quite crowded, especially during peak tourist season, so it's best to visit early in the morning or later in the evening to avoid the crowds.

ZoomTip 3.5: **Széchenyi Spa**

Széchenyi Spa is one of the most popular thermal baths in Budapest, Hungary. It was opened in 1913 and has been welcoming visitors from all around the world ever since. It is located in the City Park, close to Heroes' Square and Vajdahunyad Castle.

The Spa is open every day of the week, from early in the morning until late at night. Prices vary depending on what kind of ticket you buy, with options ranging from single tickets to package deals. A single ticket for the bath costs around 6,500 HUF (approximately 22 EUR) for an adult and 5,500 HUF (approximately 18 EUR) for a student or senior. You can also rent a cabin or locker for an additional fee. It is advisable to bring your own towel, flip flops, and swimwear, but they are available for rent as well.

The spa is famous for its outdoor thermal pools, which are open all year round. There are three large outdoor pools, including a swimming pool, and a number of smaller indoor pools. The water in the pools is rich in minerals such as calcium, magnesium, and sulfates, which are said to have a therapeutic effect on the body. The temperature of the water varies between 28-38 °C, so you can find a pool that suits your preferences.

In addition to the pools, there are a variety of saunas, steam rooms, and massage services available at the spa for an extra fee. These services are very popular, so it is advisable to book in advance. There are also several bars and restaurants on the premises, where you can enjoy a refreshing drink or a snack.

The spa can get crowded, especially on weekends and during peak season, so it is advisable to arrive early in the morning or later in the evening to avoid the crowds. Another tip is to bring a waterproof bag to keep your valuables safe while you enjoy the pools. Overall, Széchenyi Spa is a must-visit attraction in Budapest for those who want to relax and rejuvenate in the thermal waters.

ZoomTip 3.6: Callas Restaurant

Callas Restaurant is a sophisticated and elegant dining venue located in the heart of Budapest, next to the iconic Hungarian State Opera House. Named after the famous opera singer Maria Callas, the restaurant offers a refined ambiance and exquisite cuisine, which is inspired by Hungarian and international flavors.

The interior of the restaurant is beautifully decorated with classical elements, including ornate chandeliers, high ceilings, and plush seating. The atmosphere is ideal for a romantic dinner, special occasion, or business lunch.

The menu at Callas Restaurant features a selection of seasonal dishes that are expertly prepared by the talented chef. Guests can choose from a range of appetizers, main courses, and desserts, each with a unique twist on traditional Hungarian cuisine. Some of the standout dishes on the menu include the crispy duck leg confit with gingerbread and red cabbage, the black angus beef fillet with foie gras, and the caramelized apple tarte tatin with vanilla ice cream.

The wine list at Callas Restaurant is equally impressive, with a wide selection of Hungarian and international wines, carefully curated to complement the flavors of the dishes.

For those who prefer a lighter meal or a snack, Callas Cafe is located on the ground floor, and offers a selection of sandwiches, pastries, and coffee specialties. The cafe also serves breakfast, with options ranging from classic continental dishes to healthy superfood bowls.

The prices at Callas Restaurant are on the higher side, with main courses averaging around 6000-8000 HUF (20-25 euros). However, the quality of the food, service, and ambiance make it a worthwhile splurge for a special occasion.

In terms of visitor information and tips, it is recommended to make a reservation in advance, especially for dinner or during peak times. The dress code is smart casual, and guests are encouraged to dress appropriately for the elegant atmosphere. The restaurant is open daily from 8:00 AM to midnight, and free Wi-Fi is available for guests.

Top 10 Budapest Foods and Drinks to Savor During Your Visit

Below you can find our suggested local Hungarian dishes that you should try to enhance your culinary experience, while you are in Budapest.

1. Pogácsa – salty cake

Pogácsa is a type of traditional Hungarian pastry that is a must-try when visiting Budapest. It is a small, fluffy biscuit made from flour, yeast, butter, and sour cream. The dough is typically mixed with a variety of savory ingredients, such as cheese, bacon, and onions, giving each pogácsa a unique and delicious flavor.

In Budapest, you can find pogácsa in most bakeries and pastry shops, and it's often served as a snack or appetizer. They're perfect for when you need a quick and satisfying bite while exploring the city.

One of the most popular versions of pogácsa is made with sheep's cheese, which is mixed into the dough and then baked until golden brown. Another popular variety is made with bacon, which gives the pastry a rich and savory flavor.

Whether you prefer the cheese or bacon variety, make sure to try some of Budapest's pogácsa during your visit. It's the perfect snack to grab on the go, and it's a delicious way to experience a traditional Hungarian pastry.

2. Töltött káposzta – stuffed cabbage

Töltött káposzta, also known as stuffed cabbage, is a classic Hungarian dish that has been a staple in the country's cuisine for centuries. The dish consists of ground pork or beef mixed with rice, onions, and spices, all wrapped in a cabbage leaf and cooked in a rich tomato-based sauce.

Töltött káposzta is a hearty and comforting dish that is perfect for the colder months. It is often served with a dollop of sour cream and a slice of crusty bread. The dish is a great representation of Hungary's rich culinary history and is a must-try for anyone visiting Budapest.

There are many variations of töltött káposzta, with some recipes calling for the addition of sauerkraut, paprika, or even bacon. Some versions are also made with a combination of meats, such as pork and beef.

The dish can be found at many traditional Hungarian restaurants in Budapest, but it is also a popular homemade dish for families to enjoy. If you're feeling adventurous, you can even try making töltött káposzta at home using one of the many online recipes available.

When ordering or making töltött káposzta, it's important to note that it is a filling dish that is best enjoyed in moderation. However, it is a true comfort food and a delicious representation of Hungarian cuisine.

3. Etyeki wine

Etkei wine is a must-try when visiting Budapest. This wine comes from the Etkei wine region, which is located about 20 km west of the city. The region is known for producing some of the best wines in Hungary, and Etkei wine is no exception.

Etkei wine is produced using traditional techniques, and the grapes are grown in the region's unique terroir, which gives the wine a distinct flavor. The wine is typically made from a blend of grapes, such as Olaszrizling, Chardonnay, and Sauvignon Blanc. Etkei wine has a light and refreshing taste, making it perfect for sipping on a hot summer day.

When in Budapest, there are many places to try Etkei wine. Some of the most popular include wine bars, such as Kadarka Wine Bar and DiVino, which offer a wide selection of local wines. Visitors can also take a day trip to the Etkei wine region and visit some of the local wineries, such as Bujdosó Vineyard or Etyeki Kúria Winery, where they can sample the wine and learn about the winemaking process.

Prices for Etkei wine can vary depending on where you purchase it. At wine bars, a glass of Etkei wine typically costs around 500-1000 HUF (1.5-3 euros), while a bottle can cost between 2000-5000 HUF (6-15 euros). At local wineries, prices for a bottle of Etkei wine can range from 1000-10,000 HUF (3-30 euros), depending on the quality and vintage of the wine.

4. Halászlé – Fish soup

Halászlé, also known as fisherman's soup, is a traditional Hungarian fish soup that has been enjoyed for centuries. It is made with a variety of freshwater fish, including carp, catfish, and pike, and seasoned with paprika, onions, and other spices. The dish is popular in many regions of Hungary, but it is especially popular in the southern regions, where fish are abundant.

Halászlé has a distinct red color and a rich, flavorful taste. The spicy soup is often served with slices of bread or with small noodles, and it can be made with a variety of fish, depending on what is available. Some variations of halászlé include adding additional vegetables, such as peppers or tomatoes, or using different types of fish.

The dish is often associated with festive occasions, such as Christmas or Easter, and it is frequently enjoyed in outdoor settings, such as on the banks of the Danube River or at outdoor festivals. There are many restaurants throughout Budapest that specialize in halászlé, and it is a must-try dish for visitors to the city who want to experience authentic Hungarian cuisine.

5. Kürtöskalács - chimney cake

Kürtőskalács, also known as chimney cake, is a traditional sweet pastry that originates from Transylvania, but is also popular in Hungary. The name "kürtőskalács" comes from the shape of the cake, which resembles a chimney.

The pastry is made by wrapping a strip of dough around a cone-shaped baking spit, then roasting it over an open fire or in an oven until it turns golden brown. While roasting, the dough is coated with sugar and often cinnamon, giving it a sweet and aromatic flavor.

Kürtőskalács can be found in various sizes and flavors, with some bakeries offering different fillings such as chocolate, nuts, or coconut. It is a popular street food in Hungary and is often served at Christmas markets and festivals.

One can easily find kürtőskalács in Budapest, and it is a must-try for those with a sweet tooth. It is perfect for a quick snack or as a dessert after a meal. Some popular places to try kürtőskalács in Budapest include Molnár's kürtőskalács, Kürtős Kalács, and Retró Lángos Büfé. Prices typically range from 600 to 1200 HUF, depending on the size and filling of the pastry.

6. Lángos - scone

Lángos is a traditional Hungarian deep-fried dough that is very popular in the country as street food or a quick snack. It's a round, flat dough that is fried until crispy and golden brown on the outside and soft and fluffy on the inside. The dough is made with flour, yeast, salt, and water, and is then deep-fried in oil until it's crispy and golden brown.

Lángos is often served with a variety of toppings, including garlic, sour cream, and cheese, and it can be savory or sweet. It is usually sold at outdoor markets, fairs, and festivals, and is a must-try for anyone visiting Hungary.

While the toppings can vary depending on the region, some popular variations include:
- Sour cream and grated cheese
- Garlic sauce
- Chopped ham and cheese
- Sausage and onions
- Cinnamon sugar

Lángos is a popular street food and is available all year round, but it's especially popular in the summertime when outdoor festivals and markets are in full swing. It's a great option for a quick snack or a cheap meal on the go, and it's a fun and tasty way to experience a little bit of Hungarian culture.

7. Rétes - strudel

Réte is a delicious Hungarian cake that has multiple thin layers of pastry dough and filling, usually made with poppy seeds, walnuts, or cottage cheese. The cake is a traditional pastry that has been served in Hungary for centuries and is considered one of the country's national desserts.

The pastry is made with a dough made from flour, butter, and water. The dough is rolled out into thin layers, which are then layered on top of each other with a sweet filling in between. After the layers are stacked, the pastry is baked until the dough is crispy and the filling is slightly caramelized.

Réte is often served as a dessert, but it is also a popular treat to have with coffee or tea in the afternoon. It can be found in many bakeries and cafes throughout Budapest and is often served during special occasions such as weddings and holidays.

If you're looking to try réte while in Budapest, head to one of the many traditional pastry shops in the city. Some popular options include Daubner Cukrászda, Gerbeaud, and Szamos Gourmet Ház.

Make sure to pair it with a cup of coffee or tea for the full Hungarian experience.

VIIII. The Best Restaurants in Budapest

We recognize that individuals may have varying dietary requirements or preferences, so we have compiled a list of the top restaurants in Budapest. This way, you can select a different dining option from the ones we have recommended, if you so choose.

#1 Menza

This is the friendliest place on the hip Liszt Ferenc square – it offers good quality/price value, with a beautiful interior design and plenty of tables that guarantee that you can just pop in here and find a seat. The expected price for one meal plus one beer is about 3500 HUF. It is ideal for a quick business meeting or a nice lunch during sightseeing.

Address: Budapest, Liszt Ferenc tér 2, 1061 Hungary, Phone: +36 1 413 1482

#2 Bors GasztroBár

A neat little place with the best and most unusual soups in town. Baguettes, pasta, vegetable stews, and desserts are also available. Unique soup-and-sandwich combinations made of carefully selected ingredients. Daily-refreshed specials include soups and baguettes with unique flavoring, various vegetable stews, and pasta creations.
Address: Budapest, Kazinczy u. 10, 1075 Hungary, Phone: +36 70 935 3263
Site: https://www.facebook.com/BorsGasztroBar

#3 Bock Bisztró

Bock Bistro is located within the prestigious Corinthia Grand Hotel Royal, situated on the Grand Boulevard in Budapest. This restaurant boasts a rustic, yet modern take on traditional Hungarian cuisine, blending classic dishes with experimental twists. Chef Lajos Biro has a talent for reimagining traditional Hungarian meals, making them more digestible and flavorful. While on the expensive side, Bock Bistro is well worth the investment. The restaurant offers an impressive wine list and has been awarded a Michelin star for its exceptional culinary offerings.

Address: Budapest, Erzsébet krt. 43-49, 1073 Hungary, Phone: +36 1 321 0340

#4 Kőleves Vendéglő / Stonesoup Restobar
35. Kazinczy utca

Kőleves, located at the corner of Dob utca and Kazinczy utca, provides a peaceful retreat from the bustling atmosphere of the Drinking District. The restaurant serves a modern interpretation of Jewish cuisine, and its signature dish is the delicious duck breast-stake. Keep in mind that reservations are recommended, and the average cost per person is around 3,000 HUF. Although the name "stone soup" may not sound appealing, don't let that dissuade you from trying this unique dining experience.

Address: Budapest, Kazinczy u. 41, 1075 Hungary, **Phone:** +36 1 322 1011

#5 Gundel

Gundel, founded by Károly Gundel and his son János Gundel, has gained a global reputation for its opulent and dramatic style. The restaurant is situated in the City Park and is renowned for its signature dish, the Gundel palacsinta, a crepe filled with a mix of rum, raisins, and walnuts and served with a rich chocolate sauce. If you're looking to dine at Gundel, you can find it at Gundel Károly út 4, 1146 Hungary. To make a reservation, you can call them at +36 1 889 8111.

#6 Costes Restaurant

4 Ráday Street

Costes Restaurant in Budapest holds a significant place in Hungary's culinary history as the first restaurant to receive a Michelin star, a coveted recognition in the restaurant industry. The elegant atmosphere and high-quality cuisine make it an ideal choice for romantic dinners, business meetings, special events, and entertaining clients. Keep in mind that it is an expensive restaurant.

Address: Ráday u. 4, 1092 Budapest, Hungary
Phone: +36 1 219 0696
Website: http://www.costes.hu/intro.html

#7 Trófea Grill Étterem
30 Király Street

This is a fabulous buffet restaurant that offers excellent food and service, with an "all-you-can-eat" menu priced at around 15 to 20 Euros per person. To avoid any inconvenience, we recommend that you make a reservation before visiting by calling +36 1 878 0522 or booking online at Kiraly.trofeagrill.eu.

Address: Budapest, Erzsébet királyné útja 5, 1145 Hungary, **Phone:** +36 1 251 6377, **WebSite:** Kiraly.trofeagrill.eu

#8 Paprika Vendéglő

If you're looking for a place to taste traditional Hungarian cuisine, this restaurant is a great option located near Heroes Square. The interior is beautifully designed, and the portions are quite large, all at reasonable prices (around 15 euros for a three-course dinner). As it is

a popular restaurant, it's recommended to make a reservation in advance by calling 0036 20 294 7944.

Address: Budapest, Dózsa György út 72, 1071 Hungary,**Phone: +**36 20 294 7944

#9 Centrál Kávéház
9 Károlyi Mihály utca, +36 1 266 2110

The late 19th century traditional coffee house is a delightful spot to unwind while exploring downtown Budapest and immersing yourself in the atmosphere of the city's K+K monarchy era. Enjoy the best hot chocolate in town and savor a slice of delicious Dobos torte while taking in the ambiance of a bygone era. This is a perfect place to spend the entire day relaxing.

#10 Szeráj Török Étterem
13 Szent István körút

One of our preferred Turkish quick bites in the vicinity. Their offerings are always fresh, budget-friendly and available almost round-the-clock. Whether it's 3 am post-partying or any other time, you can enjoy their delightful lentil soup and tasty salads.

#11 Déryné Bisztró
$$·3 Krisztina tér

After exploring the castle district, head over to this charming and slightly upscale bistro on the Buda side. Indulge in the city's best Túrógombóc (cottage cheese dumpling) in a cozy atmosphere.

X. The 10 Best Bars in Budapest

Here is a list of the top 10 bars in Budapest, if you want to enjoy your drink in the evening.

#1 Szimpla Kert

14 Kazinczy St, www.ruinpubs.com

Szimpla Kert, also known as Simple Garden, is a trendsetter among the Hungarian ruin pubs. This legendary spot is famous among both locals and tourists. In addition to its unique atmosphere, the pub also hosts a farmer's market every Sunday, where visitors can find fresh produce, delicious meats, and cheeses.

#2 Élesztő

22 Tűzoltó Street

Located a short walk from Corvin metro station, this 3-in-1 ruin pub is a must-visit. Élesztő is dedicated to Hungarian craft beer, while Mahung offers a range of fruity cocktails, with or without alcohol. For those with a sweet tooth, Rengeteg serves up the quirkiest hot chocolate you'll ever taste. Be sure to book ahead, as it can get crowded and seating may be limited. All the beers on tap are carefully selected craft choices.

#3 Pótkulcs

65b Csengery Street

Pótkulcs is a hidden gem among the Budapest ruin pubs, with its rickety chairs, couches, and tables creating a great atmosphere for socializing. Even some locals are not aware of its existence, making it a true hidden bar. Live concerts are often held here, making it a great spot for music lovers.

#4 Divino Wine Bar

3 Szent István tér

Located in the neighborhood of St. Stephen's Basilica, this wine bar is one of the most popular in Budapest. It offers a variety of wines from all regions of Hungary, along with delicious finger food and main dishes.

#5 Fröccsterasz

Budapest, Lipótváros, 1051 Hungary

Fröccsterasz has the perfect terrace to kick off your evening from March to November. Fröccs is a refreshing blend of wine and soda, and you can bask in the sun while enjoying your drink. It's a child-friendly spot and great for groups or parties, and they offer takeaway options. The outdoor seating is perfect for people-watching and soaking up the atmosphere.

#6 Kertem

3 Olof Palme stny

Kertem is a charming open-air ruin pub located near City Park, with a cozy atmosphere that's beloved by locals. While families tend to visit during the daytime, as the evening sets in, more and more glasses of beer appear alongside the lemonades, and the Balkan Burgers become a popular choice.

#7 Ellato Kert & Taqueria

48 Kazinczy Street

This place is a unique blend of a ruin pub, a Mexican taqueria, and an open-air terrace. It also features a pool table and a large movie projector that shows films and sports events. If you're searching for an authentic ruin bar experience, this is a great alternative to Szimplakert. The signature drink is the "pinkie" cocktail, made with vodka and grapefruit juice.

#8 Kuplung

46 Király Street

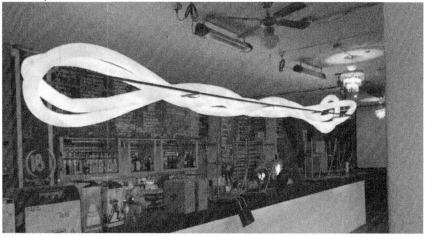

Kuplung is a large Ruin Pub that features live music events and broadcasts sports events on giant screens. The establishment has outdoor seating with long benches and unique light fixtures, such as illuminated jellyfish. To create Kuplung's unique atmosphere, a large lounge in an up-and-coming street in Pest was given to various art groups to create during the day and host events at night. Two bars were also added to the venue for visitors to enjoy.

#9 Doblo Wine Bar

Budapest, Dob u. 20, 1072 Hungary

This wine bar boasts an extensive selection, including wines from well-known wineries, as well as artisanal and organic wines and products from up-and-coming Hungarian winemakers.

#10 Kisüzem

2 Kis Diófa utca

This alternative hangout is a favorite spot among locals. The liquor selection, especially rum, is fantastic, as is the popular drink Club Mate. The kitchen serves up tasty food until about 10pm. The atmosphere is always great and it's a popular spot among artsy types. Though simple, the food is inexpensive and satisfying.

XI. The Best Shopping Places in Budapest

#1 Central Market Hall

1 Vámház körút

Great Hall Market is the most significant and oldest indoor market in Budapest, which offers meats, pastries, spices, and spirits such as paprika, Tokaji, túró Rudi, The market is closed on Sunday. Here you will find typical Hungarian products (e.g., paprika, Tokaji Aszú, Unicum, Herz and Pick salamis), fresh fruits&vegetables and souvenirs. You can also try some famous Hungarian dishes such as goulash, sausages, and lángos.

#2 Alexandra Könyvesház - Párizsi Nagyáruház

39 Andrássy út

The Art Nouveau-style building boasts elegance, luxury, and a rich cultural heritage. It houses a vinoteque, one of the largest book and music stores, and the iconic Lotz Room BookCafe at the top. It's a must-visit attraction in Budapest. The building was originally Hungary's first modern department store, featuring the Lotz Hall, a stunningly ornate Neo-Renaissance ballroom that has been transformed into a charming café.

#3 WestEnd City Center
Budapest, Váci út 3, 1062 Hungary, www.westend.hu

With more than 400 stores offering designer and casual wear, electronics, food, movie theaters, and more, this shopping center is a dream come true for shoppers. It is conveniently located next to the Nyugati Railway Station, making it easily accessible by public transportation. To get there, simply take the M3 (blue) metro line towards Ujpest and get off at Nyugati. It takes about 10 minutes. Alternatively, you can take tram line 4/6 from Terez korut until Nyugati.

#4 Sugar! Design Confectionary and Candy Store
48 Paulay Ede Street

Uniquely designed, individual sweets, cakes, quality international and home products (candies, chocolates, lollipops), designer souvenirs, sandwiches. Amusing and high-quality products.

#5 Rákóczi Téri Vásárcsarnok

Rákóczi tér

Rákóczi Square Market Hall was built in 1894. Most of the stands sell meat, although fruits, vegetables, and dining spots are also present, and there's a beauty store, and a supermarket on-site.

Fruit and vegetable market. Good bakery shop, artisan cheese. Big grocery store (Spar) inside. Open: Monday: 6am-4pm Tue-Fri: 6am-6pm Sat: 6am-1pm

#6 Great Market Hall

Vámház krt.

Budapest's Central Market Hall is the oldest and largest indoor market in the city, with a history dating back to the first mayor of Budapest, Károly Kamermayer. CNN has named it the best market in Europe, and it has been recognized as one of the most vibrant city markets on the continent. At Leves, a hipster spot in the market, you can find a daily menu featuring five different types of soup and five different varieties of sandwiches, all at very reasonable prices. "Leves" means soup in Hungarian, and it is traditionally eaten as a first course.

#7 Fény utcai piac

A friendly market where you could buy everything to eat from the farmers too. Fruits, vegetables, meat, homemade milk and cheese, jam, honey.

#8 Corvin Plaza

37 Futó utca

Corvin is one of the newest shopping malls in the heart of Budapest, behind Corvin Cinema. The 4-story mall offers a broad range of shops cafes (Costa Cafe), a CBA supermarket, cafes, and restaurants.

Thank You!

As we come to the end of this Budapest Travel Guide, we hope that it has been a valuable resource for planning your trip to this beautiful city. With its rich history, stunning architecture, and vibrant culture, Budapest is a destination that is sure to captivate and inspire you. Whether you have only a few days or a few weeks to explore this city, we believe that our itinerary, recommendations, and tips will help you make the most of your time here.

From exploring the historic Buda Castle and strolling along the Danube River, to enjoying the thermal baths and sampling the local cuisine, Budapest has something for everyone. We hope that you have found our guide to be helpful and informative, and that it has given you a good sense of what to expect during your visit.

As you embark on your journey to Budapest, remember to take your time, savor each moment, and embrace the unique experiences that this city has to offer. Whether you're here to explore the history, soak up the culture, or just relax and unwind, Budapest is a city that is sure to leave a lasting impression.

We wish you a safe and enjoyable trip, and hope that you will create many unforgettable memories during your time in Budapest. Thank you for choosing our travel guide, and we look forward to hearing about your adventures in this magical city.

Have a fantastic time in Budapest!

Your friends at Guidora.

Copyright Notice

Guidora Budapest in 3 Days Travel Guide ©

All rights reserved. No part of either publication may be reproduced in any material form, including electronic means, without the prior written permission of the copyright owner.

Text and all materials are protected by UK and international copyright and/or trademark law and may not be reproduced in any form except for non-commercial private viewing or with prior written consent from the publisher, with the exception that permission is hereby granted for the use of this material in the form of brief passages in reviews when the source of the quotations is acknowledged.

Disclaimer

The publishers have checked the information in this travel guide, but its accuracy is not warranted or guaranteed. Tokyo visitors are advised that opening times should always be checked before making a journey.

Tracing Copyright Owners

Every effort has been made to trace the copyright holders of referred material. Where these efforts have not been successful, copyright owners are invited to contact the Editor (Guidora) so that their copyright can be acknowledged and/or the material removed from the publication.

Creative Commons Content

We are most grateful to publishers of CreativeCommons material, including images. Our policies concerning this material are (1) to credit the copyright owner, and provide a link where possible (2) to remove Creative Commons material, at once, if the copyright owner so requests - for example, if the proprietor changes the licensing of an image.

We will also keep our interpretation of the Creative Commons Non-Commercial license under review. Along with, we believe, most web publishers, our current view is that acceptance of the 'Non-Commercial' condition means (1) we must not sell the image or any publication containing the image (2) we may, however, use a picture as an illustration for some information which is not being sold or offered for sale.

Note to other copyright owners

We are grateful to those copyright owners who have given permission for their material to be used. Some of the material comes from secondary and tertiary sources. In every case, we have tried to locate the original author or photographer and make the appropriate acknowledgment. In some cases, the sources have proved obscure, and we have been unable to track them down. In these cases, we would like to hear from the copyright owners and will be pleased to acknowledge them in future editions or remove the material.

Cover Photo Credit, Flickr CC: Link to Creator

Printed in Great Britain
by Amazon

20890154R00061